Amazing life cycles
MAMMALS
by Honor Head

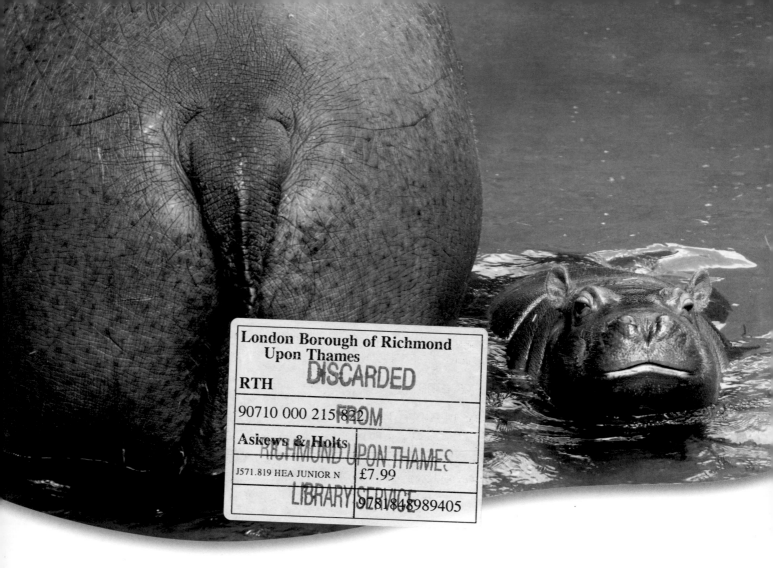

An Hachette UK Company
www.hachette.co.uk
Copyright © Octopus Publishing Group Ltd 2013
First published in Great Britain in 2007 by TickTock, an imprint of
Octopus Publishing Group Ltd, Endeavour House, 189 Shaftesbury Avenue, London WC2H 8JY.
www.octopusbooks.co.uk

ISBN 978 1 84898 940 5

Printed and bound in China
10 9 8 7 6 5

With thanks to: Trudi Webb, Sally Morgan and Elizabeth Wiggans
Natural history consultant (2013): Dr. Kim Dennis-Bryan F.Z.S
Publisher: Tim Cook   Cover design: Steve West   Production Controller: Alexandra Bell

Picture credits (t=top; b=bottom; c=centre; l=left; r=right):
Ardea: 28c. Corbis: 20 main, 21t, 31t. FLPA: 5t, 7b, 9tr, 9tl, 13 main, 15cl, 16tl, 16c, 21b, 24c, 26 main.
Nature Picture Library: 16–17 main. NHPA: 30b. Oxford Scientific Photo Library: 10 main, 17t, 18c.
Shutterstock: OFC, 1, 2, 3, 4tl, 4tr, 5b, 6t, 7t, 8tl, 10tl, 11t, 11b, 12tl, 12 main, 13t, 14tl, 14tr, 14cl, 14b, 14–15c, 15tl, 15tr, 15cr, 15b,
20tl, 22tl, 23t, 23 main, 24tl, 24–25 main, 25t, 26tl, 27t, 27b, 28tl, 29b, 30tl, 31 main, OBC.
Superstock: 4l, 9 main, 18tl, 18–19 main, 22b, 30c. Terry Hardie – www.orcaresearch.org: 8 main.
TickTock image archive: map page 6. Wendy Blanshard, Australian Koala Foundation, www.savethekoala.com: 29t.

Every effort has been made to trace copyright holders, and we apologise in advance for any omissions.
We would be pleased to insert the appropriate acknowledgments in any subsequent edition of this publication.

Contents

Words that look **bold like this** are in the glossary.

What is a mammal?

A mammal is an animal that feeds its babies with milk. Mammals are also **endothermic**. This means they are able to maintain an internal body **temperature** no matter how hot or cold the air or water is around them.

This Highland cow is a mammal.

Most mammals give birth to live babies. When a mammal baby is born it feeds on milk produced in the mother's body. This is called suckling.

A hairy hippo nose!

Mammals also have hair on their bodies. A hippopotamus is a mammal with smooth skin, but it has hair in its ears and on its nose.

The leopard cubs in this picture are suckling from their mother.

This pipistrelle bat is sitting on a scientist's finger while he studies it.

Mammals can be tiny like a pipistrelle bat, or enormous like an elephant!

Did you know that humans are mammals, too?

Mammal habitats

A habitat is the place where a plant or an animal lives. Mammals live in hot **desert** habitats and cold, icy places, such as the Arctic. The sea is a habitat. Mammals such as whales and seals live in this habitat.

Polar bears are mammals that live in the icy, snowy Arctic.

Mammals live in most of the world's habitats.

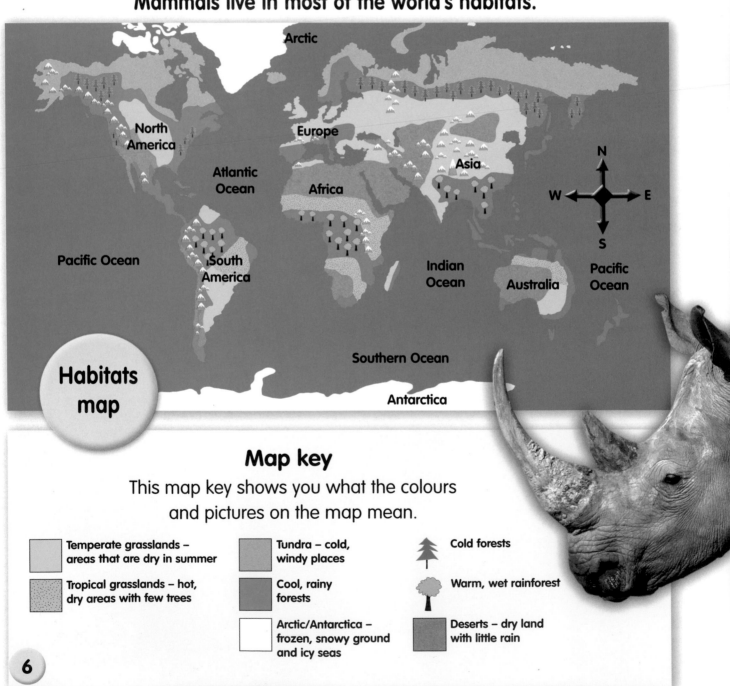

Habitats map

Arctic

North America

Europe

Asia

Atlantic Ocean

Africa

Pacific Ocean

South America

Indian Ocean

Australia

Pacific Ocean

N
W E
S

Southern Ocean

Antarctica

Map key
This map key shows you what the colours and pictures on the map mean.

Temperate grasslands – areas that are dry in summer

Tropical grasslands – hot, dry areas with few trees

Arctic/Antarctica – frozen, snowy ground and icy seas

Tundra – cold, windy places

Cool, rainy forests

Cold forests

Warm, wet rainforest

Deserts – dry land with little rain

Rainforests are warm, wet habitats with lots of trees and plants. Mammals such as monkeys, gorillas and sloths live here.

Tropical grasslands are hot all year and have a wet season. Mammals such as rhinos, elephants, giraffes and meerkats live on the grasslands in Africa.

Sloths hang upside down – the baby rides on mum's chest.

The rhino calf in this picture is suckling from his mother.

AMAZING MAMMAL FACT
Many African grassland mammals, such as lions, sleep during the day and hunt at night when it is cool.

Meat-eating mammals

Big cats such as tigers and cheetahs are carnivores.

Animals that eat meat are **carnivores**. Most carnivorous mammals have sharp claws and teeth to help them catch and eat their **prey**. Animals that hunt are called **predators**.

AMAZING MAMMAL FACT
Orcas are also called killer whales because they kill and eat seals, penguins and other whales.

Some orcas surf onto the beach to catch their prey. The waves then pull them back out to sea.

The giant anteater uses its long, sharp claws to tear a hole in a **termite** or ant nest. The insects in the nest stick to saliva on the anteater's tongue.

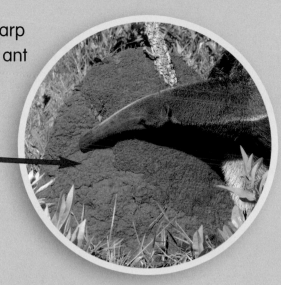

A termite nest

Bats are nocturnal. This means they sleep during the day and go hunting at night.

Many bats, including this pipistrelle bat hunting a moth, are carnivorous.

Meerkats have sharp claws so they can dig for food such as insects.

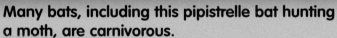

Meerkats chase and catch scorpions and lizards.

Before the meerkat eats the **scorpion**, it bites off its stinger!

9

Plant-eating mammals

A koala has several home trees in the area where it lives.

Animals which only eat plants are called **herbivores**. They eat leaves, roots, fruit or flowers. Some herbivore mammals have developed special ways to help them eat the food they need.

Hippos live in Africa. In the day they keep cool in rivers. They come out of the river at sunset to eat grass during the night.

AMAZING MAMMAL FACT
Hippos use their wide lips to grab grass. Then they swing their heads from side to side to pull up the grass from the roots.

Koalas only eat one type of food – the leaves of certain types of eucalyptus trees. These trees grow in Australia where koalas live.

Koalas spend their time eating and sleeping in the eucalyptus trees.

Warthogs are mainly grazers, but in the dry season they use their strong snouts to dig up the hard ground to find tasty underground roots.

Warthogs live on African grasslands.

Mum meets dad

Koala dads don't help care for their babies.

Some mammals **mate** and then the male and female bring up their young together. Other mammals meet, mate and then the female is left to look after the babies alone or with other females in a group.

A male and a female meerkat will become a couple. They lead a family group and generally are the only ones in the group to have babies.

AMAZING MAMMAL FACT
Meerkats live in family groups of between 2 and 50 animals.

When a male and female warthog have mated, the male leaves. Adult male warthogs live on their own.

AMAZING MAMMAL FACT
Orcas stay with their mothers all their lives. They live in family groups called pods.

When a male orca is grown-up and ready to mate, he goes to another pod and mates with a female. Then he goes back to live with his mother in his family group. Female orcas bring up their babies in their family group.

The orca couple swim around each other – it's like dancing!

What is a life cycle?

A life cycle is all the different **stages** and changes that an animal or plant goes through in its life. This diagram shows a mammal life cycle.

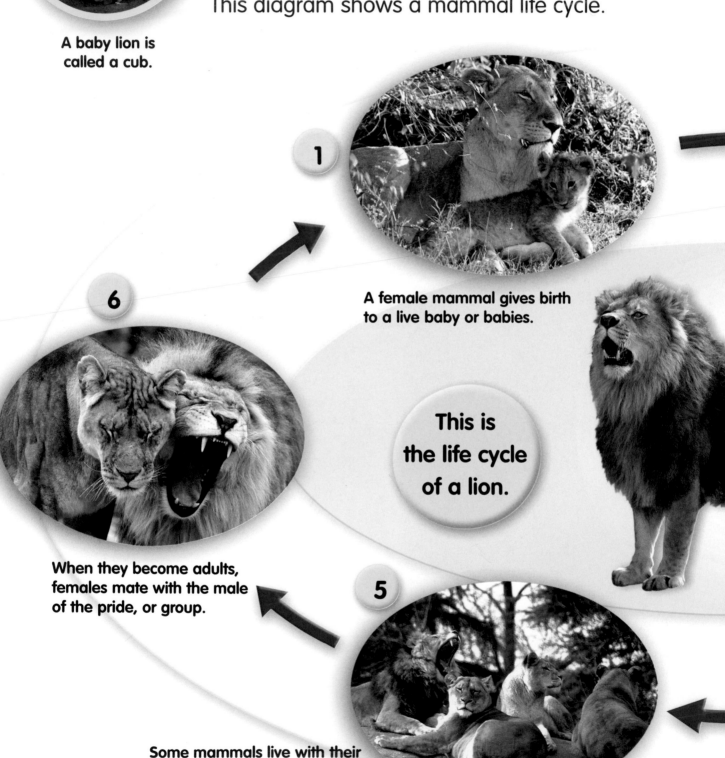

A baby lion is called a cub.

1 A female mammal gives birth to a live baby or babies.

This is the life cycle of a lion.

6 When they become adults, females mate with the male of the pride, or group.

5 Some mammals live with their family group when they grow up. Some go off and live on their own.

Amazing mammal life cycles

An orca

In this book we are going to find out about some amazing mammal life cycles – from orcas who live in the sea, to treetop koalas.

A koala

2

Female mammals feed their babies milk.

3

Lions are meat-eaters.

Mammal mothers look after their babies. Sometimes the fathers help, too.

4

Most mammals teach their babies how to hunt, or find food. Young meat-eaters practise their hunting skills on each other.

Pipistrelle bats

Pipistrelle bats usually have one baby each year. Hundreds of female bats gather together to give birth in a cave or other dark place. Sometimes they gather under a bridge or in a building such as a church or barn.

Father bats do not help look after the babies.

A baby bat is called a pup. When the pups are born the mothers and pups stay together in a huge group called a nursery roost.

Bat pup

Mother bat

LIFE CYCLE FACTS

A pipistrelle bat is usually pregnant for 50 - 55 days. A female matures and is able to have babies when she is about 12 months old.

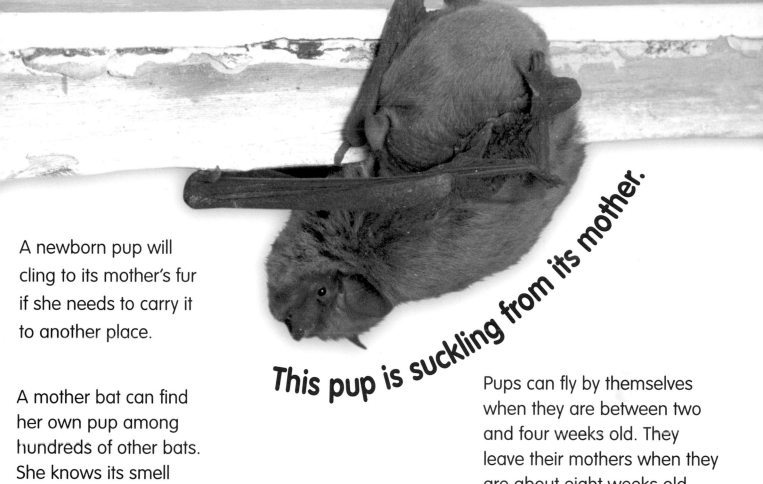

A newborn pup will cling to its mother's fur if she needs to carry it to another place.

A mother bat can find her own pup among hundreds of other bats. She knows its smell and its sound.

This pup is suckling from its mother.

Pups can fly by themselves when they are between two and four weeks old. They leave their mothers when they are about eight weeks old.

This picture shows bats in a nursery roost.

Giant anteaters

Giant anteaters live on hot, dry grasslands in South America. Adult giant anteaters live alone. When the male and female have mated, the male leaves.

An anteater's claws grow to 10 centimetres long.

An anteater can use its tail for support like a third leg.

The female giant anteater gives birth standing up on her back legs.

AMAZING MAMMAL FACT

The baby anteater is born with fur and sharp claws. It crawls onto its mother's back where she licks it clean. Baby anteaters suckle for about six months.

After a few months the baby will sometimes hop off its mother's back to explore and then hop on again.

The baby stays with its mother until it is grown-up, at the age of about two years.

If the baby falls off, it grunts to let mum know.

Orcas

Orca babies, called calves, are born underwater. They are born tail first. An orca calf can be 2.4 metres long when it is born!

A newborn orca weighs 180 kilograms.

LIFE CYCLE FACTS

Orcas are pregnant for about 17 to 18 months. A female is able to have babies when she is between 12 and 16 years old.

As soon as the calf is born the mother guides the baby to the surface so that it can take its first breath of air.

The mother orca guides the calf to the surface of the water using her flippers and her nose.

Calf

Flipper

An orca calf feeds on its mother's milk for the first 14 to 18 months of its life.

The mother orca teaches the calf how to hunt and catch food.

Orcas have pods that range in size from 15 to 52 members.

Orca families talk to each other using clicks, screams, whistles and pulsed calls. Calves learn how to make these noises.

Meerkats

Meerkats live in mobs or gangs that include males, females and babies, called kits. They live in **burrows** under the ground.

The meerkat's dark eye rings help to protect its eyes from the bright sun.

LIFE CYCLE FACTS

Meerkats are pregnant for 75 days. A female starts to have babies when she is one year old.

Newborn kits are helpless and do not have hair. They are born in the burrow and stay there until they are about three to four weeks old.

Female meerkats have two to five babies in the wild.

22

Adult meerkats take it in turns to babysit while others go out hunting.

Meerkats stand up on their back legs to enjoy the warmth of the sun in the early morning. Individuals may stand on a high point to look out for predators such as eagles.

When the kits are four to six weeks old, they start to go on hunting trips. Each kit has its own adult that teaches it how to hunt.

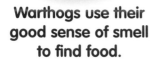

Warthogs

The female warthog may give birth to two, three, or up to eight babies at one time in an underground burrow. The babies, or piglets, leave the burrow with the mother when they are six to seven weeks old.

Warthogs use their good sense of smell to find food.

It is important that the newborn piglets do not get wet or cold. They sleep on the mother or on a raised shelf at the back of the burrow to make sure they stay dry.

Adult warthogs and older piglets enjoy a mud bath to cool off on a hot day.

Warthogs use their sharp **tusks** for fighting off predators, such as lions, for fighting each other and for digging. Both male and female warthogs have tusks.

Warthog piglets are not born with tusks. The tusks grow as the baby grows.

The piglets suckle for about four months. Male piglets stay with their mother for about two years. Females go off on their own when they are about 18 months old.

Hippopotamuses

Male hippos fight over females.

Hippos live in a group called a herd. The herd includes one adult male, lots of females and their young. When a female is ready to give birth, she looks for a soft place at the edge of the river.

If a hippo baby, or calf, is born in shallow water at the edge of the river, the mother quickly pushes the baby to the surface so that it can breathe.

LIFE CYCLE FACTS

Hippos are pregnant for 8 months. A female starts to have babies when she is 7 to 15 years old.

The mother and calf move away from the herd for the first couple of weeks. This stops the baby being hurt by accident by one of the other adults. It also helps the mother and baby bond with each other.

An adult male hippo can weigh 1,600 to 4,500 kg. The average adult female weighs 1,400 kg.

Most grown-up hippos stay in the herd where they were born. Male hippos may be driven out when they are seven or eight and eventually start their own herds.

AMAZING MAMMAL FACT
Sometimes a hippo calf will rest on its mother's back. It will slip into the water if it gets too hot and then climb back on.

Koalas

Koalas are marsupials. This means that the mother has a pouch on her tummy where her baby lives. The pouch is a bit like a pocket. A newborn koala is called a joey.

The female koala gives birth in the eucalyptus trees.

LIFE CYCLE FACTS

Koalas are pregnant for 35 days. A female starts to have babies when she is 2 years old.

This newborn joey is about the size of a jellybean.

The newborn joey is tiny! It has no hair, and its eyes and ears are not fully developed. It crawls into its mother's pouch. In the pouch the joey drinks its mother's milk.

By six months the joey has a full coat of fur. At about that time it comes out of the mother's pouch and starts to ride on her back.

Joey

At one to three years of age the koala leaves its mother. This is usually when the mother gives birth to another joey.

That's amazing!

All mammal mums care for their babies. They feed them milk and teach them how to find food. But mammal babies begin life in lots of different ways!

A baby giraffe is called a calf.

Female polar bears go to sleep in a den for the winter. They give birth to their babies, called cubs, between November and January.

The polar bear's den is under the snow. Can you see the cub?

AMAZING MAMMAL FACT
The newborn polar bear cubs are about 30 centimetres long. They are blind and pink and have very fine hair.

The mother and cubs leave the den in late March or early April.